MW01251575

DOWNRIVER

M.T. Kelly

Exile Editions

Publishers of singular
Fiction, Poetry, Translation, Drama, Nonfiction and Graphic Books

2009

Design and Composition by Digital ReproSet
Cover Photograph by permission of Elena Elisseeva / iStockphoto
Typeset in Birka and Bembo fonts at the Moons of Jupiter Studios
Printed in Canada by Gauvin Imprimerie

The publisher would like to acknowledge the financial assistance of
The Canada Council for the Arts and the Ontario Arts Council.

 Conseil des Arts **Canada Council**  ONTARIO ARTS COUNCIL
du Canada for the Arts CONSEIL DES ARTS DE L'ONTARIO

Published in Canada in 2009 by Exile Editions Ltd.
144483 Southgate Road 14
General Delivery
Holstein, Ontario, N0G 2A0
info@exileeditions.com
www.ExileEditions.com

Canadian Sales Distribution: U.S. Sales Distribution:
McArthur & Company   Independent Publishers Group
c/o Harper Collins   814 North Franklin Street
1995 Markham Road   Chicago, IL 60610
Toronto, ON M1B 5M8   www.ipgbook.com
toll free: 1 800 387 0117   toll free: 1 800 888 4741

For ~~Eleanor and Peggy~~

Jayne,

no test, in the
radiance of May

yours truly

M.T. Kelly

Terry!

2014

Downriver

The man is turning, smiling
at you from the bow of a canoe going
downriver. He is not smiling
as he has too often, too many times
in his life, telling too much: telling
everything. What you see is special,
because it's simply what a smile can be,
and special because this day, of such beauty
is the end, forever lost to him:
the snow in spring, the feeling
of being out all day in such weather;
being alone on cross-country skis,
and not being afraid: of the wet bark,
the wet everywhere, breath.

So he turns and looks back at you
and smiles, in a canoe, alone now,
but sharing all that was once out there
beyond the gunnels: the lovely silences,
the word Iroquois, his interest in
so much, what he loved, yes, loved.

The man who has become all fear
is smiling now, like never before, saying goodbye.
He is sailing into something like death,
O say it, downriver, never to see the wet spring
again, to be out, all day, in weather like this.

Danse Macarbe

The yellow skin of the bus
split like the rind of a fruit.
Fifteen bodies are scattered
on the highway. The smell of mud.

Two miles away a bear whimpers,
his nose blown off.
Children stalk birds.

The wilderness is honeycombed.
Roads form a pattern
Intricate as a brain or a cancer.

Back in the bush Cumo
and the boys used fifteen
shells. They blew the twig off.

The mine dumps seventy tons
of muck into Pike Lake.
The beaver up there is blind,
His hide's burned white.

It's country you can't walk in.
The dance will break your legs.

Mining Town

They work in the dark.
Free, they kill creatures that are
        dark, liquid as mould.
A running man sounds like an animal
        and is shot.

The forest is not virgin, nothing
        is virgin
Our remains glint
in the most secret places.
One can die out there,
        but it is not easy.

The machinery is a hymm,
like our remains, extends
everywhere, north.
Nearby a child turns evil.

There must be some revenge
in what is left, the rock
weary as flesh, the twilight.
A promise of silence.

Aurora Borealis

Hours squat like trees,
The mountain turns into a stone.
Puncturing the snow,
Alders brittle as bone.

Stumbling in this landscape
is a favour.
At least you're noticed.

Breath caresses, discolours
the purity of darkness.

A waterspout, spume
of light begins to form.
This funnel churns,
                    spreads.
The sky receives its lover.

A god is laughing.

Mountain Struck

My tendon
        rips
Each filament of
              muscle,
A carcass bright
         glistens.

Why did I climb this hill?
Drunk, I hobble and babble,
Cock a bird-blank eye,
Wait for the twisted rock,
The distancing air,
To welcome a softening body
When I am wet as moss.

Conversations

Light, pale as water,
splinters in the cold.
The sky here is glass.
Dark, when it comes,
           is rigid.
Earth collects the night.

⋆　⋆　⋆

Thirty miles south,
in a city, the city
built on rock,
a doctor speaks:

"Of course women make
good psychiatrists,"
he sniffs. The tissues
of his nose are soft.
His food is cooling.
           "That's all."

⋆　⋆　⋆

A fox runs by, leering.
A haunch drips,
      phosphorescent
in his mouth
The trees are turning
      black
Why such comfort in
those eyes? Those eyes
      alien as stars.

Killing

                Crippled,
The rabbit drags a pear-shape.
Its long hind legs are frozen,
                furred wood.

A tool necessary to finish it.
Tail lights flash, rain falls,
sand crusts the snow like a scab.
This canyon of bush could be New York;
we're alone, help waits forever.

My tire iron is new, hurry.
Wisps of hair will wash off,
Speckles of blood, like fruit.
To escape the creature elongates,
Snakes its lump into the glare.

My eye is mostly pupil,
The back's movement liquid, obscene.
A first blow twists, hits softness;
inept, there is anger, and pulp.
Sand grates metal.

I remain,
the highway, the black wall,
these waves of sentiment,
this grief.

Hawk on the Road

A sparrow, its back open, like straw.
The nodular guts look dirty, preserved.
I notice this bird while cleaning
a weapon: four feet away.

The predator has been hit, and left.
Claws, beak move; an old man whispers.
Because of thier edge I, loosely,
push aside with my foot.
Breath is indignant; a hiss and a sigh
cough from the dusty tumble.

Surely it has to be killed,
       crippled, faint movements,
          an eye popped.

My blow,
       at the tiny helmet of a head,
          tentative.

    ★ ★ ★

The eye pushes out, the bird
covers its head with a wing,
a gesture so medieval, beautiful:
I can't breathe.

The wings and feet are cut off,
not as trophies, but for magic.
Meat comes out of a leg, translucent,
warm as someone you sleep with.
Hours later the sand-cleaned steel
smells of fish.

The wings are dark, not mottled now,
There is no arc, no hiding.
      The way
            the best
                  die.

Whale Sighting: Gulf of the St. Lawrence

The river's marbled as an ancient mirror:
  Not near as old,
As the far black arms of land.

The North Atlantic, where wind can kill,
  is behind.
Now this calm, oil in the air,
Confuses us on our steel ship.

Humidity congeals like grease.

Two black shapes surface, blow,
    add mist to mist,
        return.

Their blunt heads,
    precambrian black,
        return.

The water that received them
Is great as the fluid that breaks in a birth,
    As welcoming.

How the Dolphins Came

With panic, in water too far from the island,
Plates of waves clack in the minds of the drowned.

We sail out of Notre Dame Bay, swells
pull gently on the bow. To the left,
an island, its side rotting,
seems infected with an old woman's spirit.
I imagine what could happen below,
Going over, faces turned up to the white of the sky,
Struggle becoming disbelief. Legs disappear.

Quickly they came by the blunt rusty prow,
Like sharks, but their sides had cream in them.
The bodies seem softer than rubber,
a strange kind of metal,
but skin above all,
In water that is suddenly green.

The fear their quickness causes is not revenge,
As with anything rare in nature, surprise is the first emotion.
Then comes an arc and gasp, blowholes like great soft navels
glance by the rusting steel wedge.
The function of breath is a wound.
One, then five. This energy,
this new light in the water, is reassurance.

One stays with us, froth on its back
as it breathes more quickly. Turns,
Pauses for a moment in the endless green,
Then down, down into the murk,
Down into what is to be most feared,
Down with a blessing.

Died in Childbirth: Age 22

A ruin,
  This roofless place trapped light
    Two centuries before you
      Were laid in it,
        With others,
          In Ireland.

Dust is dirty on the tomb face,
Green clutches softly in niches,
Smoke diminishes what brilliance
remains in the day.

The children were carried in winter,
Rain, famine,
Women in blankets,
Nights whose quiet breathed,
Attended you.

Twins came out.
Your hair streamed on the pillow
Your thighs were streaming,
With all irrelevant in the terrible banality of suffering

What did you see?
What purity
Turned your face wax?

⋆ ⋆ ⋆

In a nearby field a cow lies on her side,
a calf, perfectly formed,
Lies dead in a pool

Flies don't settle on her vagina
Brilliant red. They're everywhere else.
She struggles to rise.

⋆ ⋆ ⋆

The abbey is quiet now.

Your religion was cold.
The lace your sweat turned grey has crumbled.
The instruments used to open you are considered crude.

Graves point west to the dying sun.

In delirium

In silence

You stared.

Litany

The day they publised the poems about whales
two men from Brooklyn poked the eyes out of a dolphin
The paper said it cried like a baby.

A man ran over the face of a bear with a 70 horsepower
Mercury at Bon Echo. He was trying to "turn her." She
was trying to swin into the park.

Pogamiskiming: the engineer holds his bass. Between
thumb and forefinger in the jelly of the eyes. They're
going to dam the river.

According to Hemingway two gypsies killed the bull that
killed their brother by gouging out its eyes and spitting
in the sockets. They believed in honour.

In Italy hunters put needles in the pupils of decoys.
The cries of distress bring others. Canary and hummingbird
are the major game there.

Chickens in a cage, flies, a ton of wet shit, eggs and
eyes like red sores. I've seen a wild bird and a whale.
I've seen a wild bear.

The menace was a privilege.

Disappointment

The face, fleshless as a ballerina's, turns away.
Her hair has been oiled with primitive attention.
Pulled back, it exposes earings, fat and gold.
This shadow waxes her cheeks: orange tulip leaves.

Naked, Christine lifts the weight of her hair.
Her feet are mottled, hard and damp with cold.
A length of back is displayed with sly grace.
Indifference is a gift. She hopes you're watching.

Father says he'd kill for her. She thinks he should,
though his mute, scraping fingers must never touch.
Christine dances, bends, takes the shape of a bird.
It's a ritual to demand she be taken for granted.

Mother

The woman's a witch in the garden night,
Shy as a worm, weak as a dove,
Calling faintly in the dead twilight,
                              Calling...

She cries from the edge of a curving leaf,
After leaving the house as it was,
Demanding her share with miniature grief,
                              Demanding...

Little girl, little girl, with your sense of loss,
You were generous, killing—and dear.
Scream softly, echo, your wing's like a moth's!
                              Scream...

What you were when you lived inside isn't gone,
It's naked, dusted, and near.
Leave gently, part of your call was a song.
                              Leave...

The Fields of Night

Your impure body pleases
My indignant sleep.
The fields of night
          expel me

To a dry blind light
Whose bleak stain confirms
This room's neutral depth.

Your back's curve cradles warmth—
Pollen drops from your temples.

Morning burns:
        Dazed, sweetish we awaken
A film clings to our skin.
We are green and sour,
The memory of night trembles
Frail we are, and whole.

Pastoral

Your body is rocking, cool,
Bending this over roots,
Pulling up, like lean green wood
Into an arc. Shoots curl,
Humus crumbles in the lazy
Half malevolent shadow below,
White filaments twist there—
Your puckered face will blossom,
Blow into the un-subtle sun.

It's spring you see, we're locked
Here. Sealed in clear wind,
And the slopes we grow on
Could lside, boring as clay,
Chalky mud, into the valley bottom.
But it's only wind, the
Dead bright light that tells us
That. Night will find us lush,
Garlanded, glowing in the blue dark.

Euridice

The cave mouth yawns
into the waiting furnace of spring.
Surely the girl, so slender,
    Her feet unheard
Would burn in that brightness.
They must stop, and wait.

    Below, the darkness,
Green as a fly's body,
    Blue as mould,
Carries no echo

    "Euridice," he turns,
A garment, her naked body, recede.
The pure bone over sandals,
Her breasts, sweet as his own eyes,
Gone.
    And he alone,
      To live in a dream of loss,
      All we know of beauty.

Haliburton

Her hand parts a curtain,
peers out,
the house sitting on blue-veined rock.
Eighty years she's lived here,
grass and fields rich as her age,
weather sullen as her skin.

A buzz, a fly's crippled body
annoys her. She sweeps a grey
almost transparent hand.
Noise is distant, boats on the lake;
she returns to water thin depths,
the texture of her house.

Linoleum reflects her retreat
the light that follows weakens;
her room is sour, indifferent as her rage.
Outside, the rocks leak green;
the noise will bleed into quiet,
waiting; winter doesn't care.

Frederickhouse

Spruce is a green tear, between the blank lake
and sky. Blood spots blacken on the stove;
the yard is foul; a dirty porch, the bleeding
white of new wood, badly scraped pelts, no wind.

Philip Turnor named the place after a son
of George the Third. One of that family lisped,
none of them cared. Now north of Timmins the mist,
the humidity bores as it does at cottages; except
there is never any good weather here, not the way
you want it. The lakeshore, the silky water; empty.

Traders, on nearby Devil's Island, intercepted
furs on their way to Moose Fort. The Company
built this hovel to stop them. Did they dance
in the firelight there, windigo mad? I hear
the whole business became unprofitable. Both quit.

The nineteenth century: three clerks, a "number"
of natives are massacred. A blue plaque says
"the diabolical murderer Capascoos" did it.
No permanent establishment was here again maintained,
No cedar oozed wet and stink when crushed. Nothing
was unpacked.

Someone lurched, in an afternoon, lurched
and fled—dirty snow, the foul yard; blood
blackens on the stove—stopped and turned:
The clearing was mute, the sky one colour.
Scales of bark fell, left scars like new moons.
A blunt hand rested. The places hasn't changed.

Regina from the Highway

It's just another grain elevator,
Or a bleached bone,
The colour of something left behind,
Litter a century old,
Dry and friendly now,
                              like an animal skull
Discovered in a copse.

No one would have camped here,
Not in this flatness,
Valleys and rivers would have been better,
All the woods soft as beech,
Water, wind in the pale heart-shaped leaves,
But even in the hazy sunlight following the river,
Sheltered,
You'd be aware of the edge of the valley,
What was above it,
The never accepted distance in the land.

So the city's surprise,
It's not like seeing mountains,
Or suddenly, where clouds lift,
A fold, snow-veined rocks,
The Cypress Hills.

No, the city shouldn't be there,
Not like that.

I look behind, and wish for a lion on the plains.

Missinaibi

The snow curves away,
an image edges out of the swell.
A picket fence? We peer
from a cut in the tracks,
escape an edge of golden rock,
worry about darkness, getting caught.
Going over, hardwoods,
the thin trees that shoulder the town
promise an endless forest.
The picket surrounds a grave,
the grave of the first Ojibway priest
north of the great lake.
Superior, I think,
and realize where we are.

Dog Lake leads to a river and the river a sea.
This place is old, and empty.
If the tracks are black and filthy behind us,
here trains become great beasts;
indifferent, yet somehow comforting.

Missinaibi: spring that is all water and flies,
Coal oil, chill,
land always waiting for winter,
fur trade route, ruin.
Simple colours: glare or the grey sky,
black and white, and green;
green, faint green.
gold, black green.
A blocked, crude, luminous painting.
For a moment I think of dying,
a world going by, a rumble, silence again.
I am these seasons: the edge of a lake,
the pickerel spawning again;
just for a moment, I am not afraid.

All We Have

All we have in this country is landscape,
Granite shivering with light,
Winter sun, brightness that never
hints of the dark.
This place is inhabited by dreams,
The movement of glaciers.

Here the elements matter; weather,
Young trees growing in silence,
Springs violent hollow, summers breathing.
Here I stare at distant forests,
Want to receive a message;
Uninhabited landscape is a blessing.

You always invaded my search.
I remember Labrador,
Cliffs rolling their shoulders out of the sea,
St. John's, Battery Rock,
Autumn at Chaffey's Lock
when I couldn't travel, thought only of you.

In April a river seems banded by metal.
In January the disappearing twilight,
distance through trees
couldn't banish your image.
How can I blame you?
Obsession became a religion

I craved to adore,
Wished for night, your body glowing,
Wished for failure, unrelenting mystery.
A brilliant, brittle icon
suffused everything in its glow,
Even the familiar was unattainable.

But beauty's inextricably mixed with longing.
Now objects have meaning themselves, again.
There'll always be the ringing air, visions:
Impersonal life in the cold body of a trout,
A promise of happiness in a line of light,
Glimpses of a certain world, hope.

Ossossané

The bone pit, the bone pit.
These Indians lovingly re-interred
the bones of their loved ones,
buried them so Brébeuf could watch,
and the site,
is 250 yards behind a sign.

To reach the place I ski into
a blood-red sun,
through a dark forest;
I'm on water, I'm on ice,
only to reach an ordinary
clearing, and fear a barking dog.

The field is dull,
wire nailed to boards, a cattle chute.
Yet here, for the first time in Canada,
the past exists.
Here in the commonplace,
by a curve of dead cedar.

A rabbit crosses my vision.
Obsessed, head tilted as if concentrating,
the creature mocks me.
I hear no voices from the feast of
the dead,
feel only my feet, the cold.

It's kind of a miracle,
the colour of bones:
globes on a fenur, wood and bone.
What pierces me now will always ache,
and I turn to flee,
into the present, into the known world.

The pain will pass,
the countryside changes;
but there is such a thing as haunting.
Here something happened.
Here was something else.

Death occurs.

Manitoulin, Going Home

The strait is behind us, and whatever lives
below the black water
feels the peace of centuries again.
As we crossed to this island something stirred,
a memory of the south; Wenroronon, Tionnontaté,
lines of captives with smouldering hands.
The plain of the lake shivered, and below each wave,
far down, a single presence shrugged,
mourned, thought of escape.
Then cries came from the east,
The Dispersal of the Huron,
refugees eating corpses, the wet slush of a spring
three hundred years ago.
I can feel what went on, you said,
but we're in the north now.
The limestone landscape will change,
and cedars in a field, mist over marsh hay
are personable, small.

Tomorrow,
Clearwater will be a daylight village,
will shine in the vast narrows,
but we'll still go on;
travel to where we can hide behind rocks,
to where uninhabitable country stretches
green and alien as a dream.
We're together you and I, going in:
Wife, mother, let us forget memory,
but remember this young country,
the cold pure air, distance and rivers.
Virginity is only an idea,
but here we do have innocence;
We're going, not to a place, but home.

The Broch of Gurness

A hand with a ring was found in a midden heap.
Here are cattle, trenches, a rubble of stone.
These people, we are told, made a living
from the harvest of the ebb tide flood;
that is, the women gathering whelks, and something
cut from the wrist of a young girl
was tossed among the clam shells.

Suddenly, in the ocean, heads appear.
Silkies! No, just sea mammals,
part of the bay,
the promise of the outer islands.
Orkney's fields glow; there's russet, turquoise,
cliffs and rain.

That's how the legend started.
Silkies are someone to trust.

Dachau Concentration Camp

Only one detail makes any sense.
In the barracks, each bunk has a little ledge,
separating it from the other.
These tiers, these boxes *have* to be human!
I could hide behind the six-inch rampart,
—in the pile be private, be cozy.

There is a rack on each tray of the crematorium,
for bodies. Because of its dimensions,
a furnace edge has echoes of the personal;
is a lie, like hope.
Below were gas rooms for corpse piling, storage,
which now smell like a cellar, mildew, urinals.

Outside is the richness, the damp of a European
forest: moss on the black earth, a garden,
a purling stream, the gods that have gone.
All are meaningless.
Here was an absolute ending.
The purling stream becomes a ditch.

After the God

He's very quiet, you said, meaning dull,
the man you're going to marry;
and no matter what the shadows promise,
nothing is transformed.
Everyone can claim a kind of innocence.

What matters is that images linger;
one humid night, two women,
a dream that was a prayer:
the boreal forest in winter,
a glade at the edge of the world.

A god inhabits them all,
A god of high spring sky,
Of April and May light:
There's a shimmer
in this haunted wood.

What gleams repeats,
The god will come again.

Riverdale Zoo Is Closing

Smoothing for six months
A foul half-moon curve
With his soft cracking paws,
Souring the concrete
Spoiling it like damp rot
In the angle of a basement,
His snake head grins and rises.
The polar bear's lips are pulled
In a dog's consoling stretch
The tender edge familiar
But the scalloped line is blank
Drawn with an idiot's strain.
His eye is white and turns
A circle blue as opal
The intimacy of an element
Ice melting dark as earth.

The rest of the zoo's below;
Exotic birds, flamingos
Rigid in a swamp
Dingy, tinged they stand
Central in stagnant pools.
Two pelicans have growths
Wood twisting on their bills.
Paper cups and refuse
Hide in every corner
But green can gather still
Where willows breathe completely
And trees can flower in twilight
Over cunning fences
Up the slope, dank bunkers,
seeping black, abandoned
by the massive breathing light.

The Day

for Lynn King, April 1944 – March 2005

The day the word death was used
"I want to live," you said.
Not "to see spring again" or
"to stop the suffering" (words
others offered), but surely for those
gestures which, unique to you,
like wearing lovely navy colours
on a leaden day, cast a shattering gleam
off yet another steel procedure.
It was heraldy, it was grace;
Your bravery, our smiles.

December

Now the uneasy hour,
The wastes of night sail by;
High windows glower,
Red from a winter sky.
Hedges touched in snow.

No shiver wakes the spine,
Just cold, and what we know:
This is the month of solstice,
Rose in that raw glow.

Arctic Blue
for Max

Once is a decade, no,
not in a lifetime, ever,
this blue, in spring light
over snowdrifts in the
same yard that one green
summer, your mother
gardening, you grew in.

The gold fire of a child is
now a shadow, evergreen:
black spruce, high latitudes,
Such cold, such
lengthening light, where
you were, and will be
again, and always.

Shoreline, Old Lake Iroquois

Here ice melts, the mineral water,
holds all light lacking in the sun.
We slide under; the road,
the forested slope becomes shoreline,
the glacial drop of an ocean lake.
It's so clear in the shallows—
only the rainbow flash of a trout—
until we go deeper; forever,
there is nothing but dark.

Stay near the surface,
breathe the bright water,
all is magic: leave
your clothes, wet furs rotting in a pile,
fire-sharpened sticks,
your body.
Leave the smooth stones
in their
vision pits.
Leave: weather that will stay bad
for ten thousand years;
pebble beaches, campsites,
the violent sky, dread.

The Withrow Site
Withrow and Broadview

The lake's metal shone in the distance
a dream of menace.
Even in sunlight, the valley's slope
down to the river, a huge flank,
was protection:
And above the old corn,
the April, a thousand years ago,
the sky led to an endless west.
Behind the village another valley
guarded the east,
where a stream sang in the afternoon.
Outside the palisade—the bark damp—
all was still.
Only the smell of fish, smoking and rotting
foretold any future, and that
quickly passed into silence:
no one, nothing moved.

II

The lake still shines with menace,
but now it's dead,
The valley sneaks up the landscape
an artery of green,
an illusion of quiet in this city,
shimmering.
The slope that leans east has no stream,
What's left is hidden, cowering
underground,
not hiding like an enemy,
waiting for ambush and return,
but just waiting,
hoping for light, and the sky
on this site,
this place of old life,
extends far into the blue,
in April abundant.

Child and Petroglyph
for Jonah

Hair the colour of pollen and sunlight,
cry high and faint as a bird,
the child runs across drying marsh;
the empty forest carries no echo
of his song. A tiny, solitary plover,
here from the Arctic, darts
beside him, matches his beauty on the
mud flats, as eager, as lovely. Turning,
they both look at me and the little boy asks,
"What comes at night?"

We turn to leave this place
of trails and stone carving.
It is autumn, it is evening, and the old
religion, all religion
seems based on one thing: fear.
There are spirits here, and they
are not benign.

Because the stone heaves in the night,
and Misshipizhu breathes,
fissures in the earth, in a body,
crack and open;
a snake dances, lays eggs,
an overloaded canoe
filled with stick men
dips into another world.
There is a voice under the rocks;
and quartzite, fading light, silence.
There are all these things,
the ancient darkness, this child, this radiance.

The Voyage, Beginning

Until my father died just after my eighth birthday, and for a few years after that, we lived in an area of Toronto known as the Junction.

I was born on November 30, 1946, and trains were a factor in my childhood, even if I could not see, nor do I remember hearing them, from the one-bedroom apartment over a cigar store that I shared with my mother and father: 3103 Dundas Street West.

One of the memories I have of my father is his taking me to the Lampton roundhouse and putting me up in the cab of a steam locomotive. In a hallucinatory way I even remember being in one moving: fire, and the light of a very bright day, the men shifting about, a platform swaying. To this day trains reassure me in a profound way: I explain it now by describing trains as great benign beasts, monsters who will not hurt you: all this associated with a father.

There was anxiety too about going to the roundhouse, because we just walked in there and I feel, even then, that I worried about it. But as my mother has said, my father could "turn on the charm," everyone liked him, everyone liked Milt, and I do know that that is one of the reasons we could walk in there and have me lifted into the cab. My dad in a suit, my dad who could talk to anyone. Many years later I was told how he even had Ernie the landlord "eating out of his hand."

That apartment was important. It was only two stories, and as you entered our unit there was a bathroom to your right, a long hall with a living room and a bedroom side by side facing the streetcars of Dundas: opposite them a large kitchen leading out to the back and an iron fire escape enclosing a U-shaped court and facing "the lane." I once tried to go back and look at the place but was met by a man nearly insane with anger and suspicion who would not let me in. I saw significance in the man's rudeness; he was an immigrant, and an echo from childhood came back: the "Maltese had driven us out." The man, however, was simply a paranoid jerk. Had I gotten into the place, the well-known but still constantly surprising recognition − not so much of things being smaller but, what is harder to acknowledge − of you being bigger would have applied. In the end it is what happened then and what I remember − that has had such power.

I had no room of my own but a cot at the foot of my parents' bed, beside the wall, near the door. After my father died, the cot disappeared and I shared my mother's bed. I shared it before he died, as I remember being in bed with my mother and his coming home one night and putting a wrestling hold, a leg lock, on her. He must have been drinking, and the kind of joking he intended was the kind that went with a grin with a cigar stuck in it. I remember her whisper, "He'll kill us, he'll kill us," her nightgown, and a shriek.

Another time I was frightened was when my father sat on the side of my cot and I knew he had been drinking and he sang, I think it was, "Auld Lang Syne," and would not stop when my mother told him to, and the next day my father knelt and apologized to me in the kitchen: the kitchen with its yellowish walls where he used to have "doubles" and "singles" – bread folded over, dipped in tea. The kitchen where he carried a fridge up the fire escape, and slapped me one time for having different coloured socks on; it was the place I left to go and buy steak for one of my mother's boyfriends after my father died. My mother was struggling with money and I was very aware of it, and when I came back with cheap round steak instead of T-bone, and this was a chance for T-bone, there was disparaging laughter. I've heard the sound of that laughter in my stories since.

When he died, my father was a "customer's man" for a brokerage company. He had had many jobs. He knew some rich men and I met one of them. My mother had started a company called "Bridal China and Crystal" before he died and carried on with it after his death. She later got a job in a brokerage office herself, selling over the phone. There was never much money, and I was always aware of it.

In that apartment I waited for Santa Claus, seeing yellow light on snow on a deserted Dundas Street on Christmas Eve, and it was looking down the long hall of that apartment – railroad halls, they called them after Pullman cars – coming home with my mother happy after Christmas shopping, the freshness of the outside still on us, that I saw my father dialling for an ambulance that would take him away to die.

In writing this I am able to recall, perhaps for the first time, how sick he looked: am I half imagining, half seeing, how his always large forehead stood out? At last I deduce, over forty years later, that he was small from cancer; until this moment he had always seemed big. And what surprised and alarmed me because it disrupted things – his fumbling at the phone, looking at us with what I thought then was unnecessary crisis – I see now as shock and desperation. He knew he was going to die. Years later I saw a letter to him from his relatives in New York, which I think talked about his needing a miracle – it acknowledged his condition. But that moment: his eyes, looking at us. They were brown, dark, so big. I had forgotten his eyes. He and my mother used to talk and sing about eyes, hers were blue: "Beautiful beautiful brown eyes." My father's mouth, the thin Irish frog mouth: grim. So familiar now. How I remember things about my father, the optimism I had to make myself feel on a sunny September afternoon as he drummed his freckled hand on the arm of the car seat – we had a new car, a '54 Ford. We were waiting outside a hospital. His hand.

So much comes back. Holding tight to his pant leg when he asked me how I would feel if he had to go away on a trip. I don't even know if I knew the word, but I knew that this was about death, about him going away and never coming back.

Images, childhood scenes that emerge in your adult stories. Being in Grade Three and looking up at the classroom clock and thinking, now, this time of the morning, he is having his operation.

He got sick. He was sent home from the hospital for Christmas. I remember taking the turkey carcass into his bedroom after Christmas dinner. I know I wanted him to examine it with me in some happy scientific way: "Get it out, get it out, get it out, get it out!"

After all those years I conjure up so much, the details: his pyjamas and oxblood slippers. It is uncanny how the moments come back.

It's what comes back that can give a singular tone to a storyteller's stories: the phone table where my mother sat when she told me my father had died, a brilliant January day; and somehow I thought I was going to receive news that he was having a bath. Then the crying and crying.

Writing this has allowed me to see that time and place; almost to re-inhabit my small body. It is a profoundly uncomfortable feeling, and I must reassure myself that I can leave some of me and the past behind. I must also not assume the connections I make will have the resonance for others that they do for me; but then, writing is always an act of faith in others' imagination.

Baths. Because kettles had to be heated for bath water in that flat – and one of the few times I was left alone with my father he gave me a bath, and then he punished me – baths were significant. I recall the knobs of my mother's spine when I sat behind her in the bathtub and bathed with her. So many of my frantic feelings, so much of the agitation of that place, along with the grief and terror, come back. I remember walking down that long long dim corridor after the bath with my father. He was behind me, and swinging his belt; then, lying across my parents' bed; the empty dark air, the space of the room above me: the detonating crack of the strap, across the bedpost. He hit it repeatedly, not me.

Well before I was nine, I know I was sick of that Junction apartment and neighbourhood – it had changed. I had known for a long time it was over for me, that special places were too small now, and had no magic left in them. I was glad when we moved, although we moved to another similar one-bedroom apartment, this time a high rise in Parkdale. The grief of my father's death, so intense, would last and last, and aspects of it must last still. I remember forming an imaginary Club of always victorious heroes, using his initials, the MTK's. And when I heard "Danny Boy" I would weep. But I grew and when I was about twelve or thirteen I got my own bed and my own room. The numbers of the apartments where we lived are like names to me, and I can tell them over and over again: at 60 Tyndall Avenue in Parkdale we went from apartment 302, one-bedroom, to 708, two-bedroom, to 901, two-bedroom. It was the same building my mother's boyfriend lived in. We were permanent. But transient! I did not live in a house until I was an adult.

Parkdale and the Junction were different neighbourhoods. Parkdale is located in the west end of Toronto and used to be connected to Lake Ontario through Sunnyside, an area south of Parkdale that bordered the lake and served as an amusement park. This world of shore-front dance halls and ferris wheels all ended in the '50s when the Gardiner Expressway's great trench and elevated concrete skyway cut the neighbourhood off from the lake. Parkdale was also one of the first areas of the city to experience massive high-rise development. The Junction had, by and large, remained what it was – an old neighbourhood, one-storey apartments over stores facing a busy street. No trees. Threadbare. Poor, really. From the Victorian to '40s architecture. Brick. There were houses on the streets off Dundas, some working-class on the British model, some finer. Mansion houses on High Park Avenue, two blocks away. The Junction was almost entirely Anglo-Saxon, but during my childhood it was certainly said disdainfully that "the Maltese" (who were often Pols and Ukrainians) were moving in and changing things. I was changing myself, very much outgrowing the place. How glad I was that we had moved, when I was in Grade Five.

There seem to me now to be certain themes, in both the Junction and Parkdale that give a feeling of the places. But these themes are also about my own psychic geography as well,

One of these themes was fighting. The Junction was perhaps more poor than tough, but my father had boxing gloves in the house and he brought home a boy for me to box, or fight with in the living room. I half remember the chesterfield, the furniture: I remember swarm, the punching. He was a smaller boy, and I felt guilty about winning. There was also, however, a fight – outside where the courtyard joined the lane – with someone "tougher," that my father watched from the top of the fire escape and did not interfere in. I wish he would have. I vaguely recall conversations about me doing okay and that it was understandable that I did not cry until I walked up the fire escape to get near him – but I didn't like the whole thing. The names of the boys I fought and played with are clear. I can recite them, like the ringing of a bell, but I will not list them here. After he died I found a book of my father's, a book about self-defence that had in it the technique for gouging out an eye.

In Parkdale, too, there were fights as well. Fighting was very important. My best friend was Jack Moore, from Cape Breton, who ended by dying violently. I met him after I beat up his brother. Jack came and beat me up. I went back to fight him, having read books about animals fighting to inspire myself, but made friends with him instead, and he didn't admit, or know, it was me who he had beat up. We pretended we were "tied" in fighting. That became our story. I didn't have to fight the guys he had "taken." The permutations of this story were unending, but I remember them. I wrote about Parkdale and its fighting, and glue sniffing, and ambience in my play *The Green Dolphin*.

So much of where we have been, and of what has happened to us we recreate as legends or myths whose meaning is received; part of a way in which we see and explain ourselves. I know the stories I tell, and have told of my old neighbourhood, are like that. Our narrative may not always take in other dimensions. For instance, Parkdale was certainly distinctive in Toronto in the sixties for the emphasis it placed on rhythm and blues music. I once wrote:

> In spite of the devastation, the denizens of Parkdale have always had a special sense of themselves as a neighbourhood, which sense continues to this day. In the mid-sixties, Parkdale supported a subculture which many par-

ticipants thought to be unique. While other teenagers looked to the Beatles, "the boys" (and girls) of Parkdale looked to black rhythm and blues and listened to Buffalo radio stations, such as WUFO. They dressed in clothes which, as one of their girlfriends commented, "made them look like apprentice pimps": stovepipe pants, silk and wool suits. They carried umbrellas. "The boys" had "Twist and Shout" by the Isley Brothers years before it was recorded by the Beatles. No one had a car, and the centre of this world was The Green Dolphin Restaurant.

This was true enough, but there is much more to it than that, and it was not as special as I thought. It was the people who were unique, not the sociology; if anything, what lights up a place is a certain timelessness in history, its ghosts, combined with nature, or what remains of it, and the present.

Naturally I made a legend of my father, and my mother encouraged me. She could never marry again, she would say, I was so sensitive. Without giving away too much, it is fair to say I became very special to her, a kind of husband – we had a "special" relationship, while she also had boyfriends.

Later, I found out things about my parents that were surprising, not like the legend or the terrible grief of a child.

At his death my father was fifty-eight, at least twenty years older than my mother. He could do "a hundred push-ups," swell out his chest so that milk bottles could be placed on it. He did this at parties, I was told. And every picture I have of myself in grade school shows a child, a year ahead in school because of his November birthday, small for his age, with his chest puffed out like a pouter pigeon. My father dressed "immaculately," and I do remember the smooth, nearly chamois-like quality of a beige sports shirt he had. Something of that shirt, a sliver of memory, still has in it weeping and love. He smoked White Owl cigars. He didn't want to take me, and only did once, to the women's softball he watched at Sunnyside in the evenings. His excuse was that all I wanted to do was eat. I think now, what else is new? All kids are like.

Some research that I have done (unlike my mother's stories of how "they came from the County Claire" told in a rising voice, or of how "they came from the Isle of Mann") revealed that my father's paternal grandfather came from Ireland and settled in Markham Township, northeast of Toronto. My father's father was born there in the countryside — there were five children, two born in Ireland, three in Canada, to William Kelly, Labourer, RC, and his wife Bridget – but moved to Toronto quickly. I know very little about him. I think he worked for the transit company. My father's mother's maiden name was McInerney.

My father himself was born in the east end of Toronto in 1897, Milton Thomas Kelly, one of eight children, two of whom were stillborn. He had been married once before he met my mother and had lived in New York for a time. As a child I visited that city where I still had Irish relatives and remember walking through a tough neighbourhood with my father. Again he wore a suit. There is a picture of this. I'm sure I was told to walk slowly and not to be anxious, not to worry. I'm sure I worried. I remember my father as big.

From this first marriage, which I didn't learn about until I was nearly twenty, I have a half-brother named Ray. He was born in 1922 and I have never had any contact with him. The information was kept from me, I'm quite sure, so that the ideal I had of my father, and was encouraged to have, would not be spoiled.

Once my father had separated from his first wife (Ruby Smail, the spelling may be wrong), he came back to Toronto with the son, who was shifted about to live among my father's sisters. That must not have worked because eventually the boy went back to New York with his mother. My own mother saw this child once, my father asked her to find him in New York, and confronting Ray at a schoolyard she asked him if he wanted to see his father. Ray asked her "Why?" I am told Ray's mother moved after that and my father could never find the boy. A connection broken.

On his return, my father lived in Toronto with different sisters, Margaret, or "Ummie," or Rhea, and he was living with the youngest, Doris or "Doe," and her husband and children when he met my mother.

My mother had always been secretive about her age, but she was born in St. Catharines, Ontario, one of three children, all girls. Her father, Harold Preston Vores (1880-1945), had attended Cambridge and lost much of his inheritance, and in Canada, among other things, ran a candy store. He married my grandmother, Lucy Annie Jones (1879-1965), daughter of a stonemason, a skilled craftsman, in Toronto in the late 1800's. My grandfather was a member of the Masonic order. It is on his tombstone. There is a genealogy on my mother's father's side, going back to John Preston of Norwich, England, 1587-1628. The first name listed in the genealogy is Thomas Preston "of Norwich, published *Canabosis*, 1570." Another source has him listed as "Cambridge, England, 1537-98, published *A lamentable Tragedie, mixed full of pleasant mirth, containing the life of Cambises, King of Persia* (1569)." Canabosis and Cambises are so close, as are the dates, 1569 and 1570, I am sure it is the same person. My mother was much interested in such things, though I was deeply aware that her boyfriends, after my father's death, were not aristocrats.

I looked for father figures and didn't have too much luck. At Lake Simcoe, north of Toronto, which I visited with my mother and her boyfriend Lorne Scobie, I remember being allowed to sit for an hour on the dock and fish with Steve Rocco, an ex-boxer and bookie. We talked. He'd fought Frenchie Belanger three times and contended for the Flyweight Championship of the World. He was a soft-spoken man, but I remember the wonder, and wonder still, when he told me that before his fights no one could believe his heart rate didn't go up. He also told me, a gentle aside crossing his wide, warm face, that it was not a good job being a bookie "because it was so hard to collect." We caught bass. Small ones. I will never forget his dock, or how he looked slouching a little over the water as I went to sit beside him. He held my hand once. I will never forget Mr. Rocco.

"Scobie" became the man in my mother's life. "Uncle Scobe" who bragged he was only a truck driver but nonetheless a millionaire. He did not appreciate "perfessers – perfessers a' nothin'!" like me. The stage was set for many dramas with the ghost of my father, Uncle Scobe, and my mother's talk of my sensitivity. There were instructions on how to manipulate Scobie – such as calling him "Uncle Scobe" – and who, I was informed, had very clean underwear for a bachelor. A shorthand I use to characterize my mother's and my interactions with Scobie is jesters dancing around the court of an insane king, who would rouse himself occasionally to mutter, "I don't give a shit."

We, my mother especially, would become more hysterical and frenzied around him. Yet for all her hysteria she was absolutely immovable and unchangeable in her methods and purpose. My mother had what I referred to as Nietzschean will. Implacable. She did not listen. She got her way.

After Scobie's death I came upon one of his business cards: Lorne (Buff) Scobie, with telephone numbers on one side and a joke about women on the other so vulgar it can't be published here. He died of cirrhosis of the liver, he was up to forty ounces of rye a day. Once Scobie bought one of my girlfriends, and my mother, "hot pants." I remember him referring to my mother as "that little girl." My father may have done the same. Decades later I found a note from him referring to "A PRESENT for the best little girl in the world."

The drama of childhood is only part of the picture. I do know that very early I went to an imaginative world. This was about knights and armour, trains, and most strongly, animals and wilderness. Not that we had a cottage or that I went to camp, or ever experienced the wild – there may have been one visit to Georgian Bay to a cousin's cottage where my father made a battleship out of a two-by-four, and there was a story of how I burnt myself on hot coals at a Great Lakes beach – but my imagined experience was very real. I can remember discussing why I liked Ernest Thompson Seton's work over that of Sir Charles G. D. Roberts with Miss Alice Kane, the librarian at Lisgar Library in Parkdale. That kind of library is gone now, serious libraries with well-made hardbacks in open stacks. How I remember the way some of the books were made, how they smelled and looked and felt and were illustrated. The world of the imagination, and of the imagination combined with reading, was so powerful.

After my father's death I was sent to a Catholic school, De La Salle, staffed mostly by violent, strap-wielding Christian brothers. This was the Catholic order which figured in the extreme sexual abuse of children at Mount Cashel orphanage in Newfoundland. But Brother Richard, in Grade Four, was not like that; as I remember him, he was extremely aloof, and orderly, and exactly what I needed. Then, I had a warmer teacher in Grade Five, Brother Terrance, perhaps the best year I ever had academically. I remember reading a high school text, *Ancient and Medieval History*, right through in that grade, and I read it with enormous pleasure. Also, stories of the Jesuit martyrs sparked my life-long interest in native peoples. And I had been to the Martyrs' Shrine early in life: the broken wall in a farmer's field, piled stones, all that was left of the old mission.

Then, there was the lane behind the apartment building, empty. I recall aspects of its silence on a summer afternoon, cinders catching the sun. If there were a child's cries in that place, they are faint now, as of birds in the wind.

There was a musty garage, and garage roofs that gave access to trees in someone's backyard, climbed furtively. There was a broken fence, black mud and puddles, the light in the nuggets of dead coal. I would go on bike-riding adventures on St. John's, where trees overarched, oily leaves from dark maples, great black trunks indifferent and comforting. The memories are mostly of summer, but snow as well, no March light that would figure so prominently in my life in Toronto in later years. What there was of spring was the space between the trees in High Park before the grass had colour, spring clothes, even the idea of which still gives me a headache, and talk of the Easter parade; empty, open, dusty spring, no lavender light, no sense of possibilities. That would come later. Some of these memories must have led to what I have written about and felt, to what I finally saw in the the new green on tundra hills, to the comfort I took: peace.

Whatever connection I had to the natural world was through dogs. I had a few dogs, read dog stories, and one dog in particular, which did not last long and was returned to the pound, seemed significant to my imaginative world. I named him Buck, after Jack London's *Call of the Wild*, which I read early. I used to fight him, in a truly obsessive, repetitive way in the downstairs corridor of the apartment building. That tunnel, dark, all of it shiny, as if even the walls were waxed, hardwood floor and linoleum, became a complete wild world. I was also influenced by Roderick Haig-Brown's *Panther*, but what was significant was an incredible, isolate, lonely interacting with the dog. There was a feeling-sorry-for-myself sweetness, combined with a lonely yearning; as well as a deliberate craziness, going into another space or dimension. It wouldn't be accurate, however, to say that this was the beginning of fantasy – as expert as I would become at fantasy – because for all the isolation, the time-out against the world, just me and the animal, I was looking for some kind of real connection.

The dog that we did manage to keep the longest was heartbreakingly stolen from me when I tied him up outside the Riverdale Zoo, to which I had gone alone. Animals.

The first poem I ever wrote and published was titled, "Riverdale Zoo Is Closing," full of intense compassion for a psychotic polar bear.

My first literary experience – it's an inexact label but comes close, perhaps I should say self-conscious epiphany – occurred in the corner of the De La Salle school library. This library stressed such books as the Hardy Boys mysteries, there wasn't much, but they had *The Old Man and the Sea* by Ernest Hemingway, perhaps thinking it was a safe book. I clearly remember holding the book and reading the opening paragraphs. That moment. Here, I must have felt, was dignity – here was how to be in the world. A definition I have of literature that I came to like was that it was good advice touched with a breath of beatitude. I had thought it was something like that very very early: how to live.

At De La Salle I had good instincts about how not to live, and I knew it was time to get out. At De La Salle there was a football team; at the public high school, Parkdale Collegiate, there was swimming, gymnastics, and especially track and field. At De La Salle there was a drum and bugle corps run by Brother Xavier, nearly psychotic in his explosive violence; at Parkdale there was a symphony orchestra. And most importantly, Parkdale was co-educational, so I went there.

I settled down, and with the help of two very good teachers I wrote a story that tries to recreate some of the feelings of what went on at Parkdale: "All That Wild Wounding".

All That Wild Wounding

Wind, stopped by tall buildings, blew down across construction sites and parking lots. The confused air then swirled and climbed again, gritty in the twilight. Those people who were walking turned their heads aside, grimacing. The cold blue of March light, high up, seemed improbably far away, part of another world.

Inside the convention centre there was no hint of weather; just a subdued murmur as two or three hundred people lined up for drinks and waited for the dining hall to open. Yet somehow, in the hush and noise of growing talk, in spite of carpet and ventilation systems, escalator motors and voices, David was aware of dirt and storm. With a chill he knew it was now dark outside as he turned to listen to Theresa.

"The women seem to have done so much better than the men." Rolling her eyes in a round face, glancing but never looking at him, Theresa talked in a way all too familiar after twenty years. No matter what she said it was though she was letting him in on a secret.

She shared the facts – and the men, balding, paunchy, did look worse than most of the women – but at the same time let him know he was supposed to be shocked. The contrast was between her directness and her little girl's voice.

"Well, yes…" Looking around, not knowing where to go, David moved his eyes from Theresa's face to her dress. It looked as if she'd just stepped off the top of a wedding cake, but the colour of the bunching, billowy satin was the green of a hospital corridor or vice-principal's office, places where he'd spent hours, waiting.

"I love reunions, don't you?" she said.

"Neither of us has been to one before," he said. "Have you? We're not that old."

"But the school's a hundred! And just seeing everybody…" The cute warmth with which Theresa said "everybody," as if she was saying "ahhh" to a puppy or infant, was stubborn. David felt she would not stop, wouldn't drop her attitudes. Her eyes rolled away again.

One of the first things Theresa had let David know was that she was in commercial real estate; filling him in on how she was doing. He didn't know whether to believe her, though it was probably true: still, it was part of her armour. He could tell just by looking how some of the others were doing, without waiting for them to say things like "my company" within ten words of "hello." So David told Theresa he'd heard Gutwinski was also in commercial real estate, just like she was. "Old Gut," he said.

"Ahhhh," she purred back at him.

Suddenly David felt poisoned by the expected. He wasn't bitter, and didn't bore himself by asking "Why did I come?" But the utterly closed faces around him, even the sad, expectant ones, products of time and divorce, were disheartening.

Music came on, a rhythm and blues record from their era, "For Your Precious Love." The song was haunting, so suffused with grief that it pierced him.

"God, I hate that music," he said. "We used to think we were so special because we liked rhythm and blues." He shook his head.

"I love it. I still love it." Theresa brightened up. "It's the rhythm. It is! The rhythm. I can't listen to a song, even today, if it doesn't have the rhythm." She was really enthused, as if she'd discovered something.

"Do you want to dance?"

When she was in his arms, her dress crinkling, the smell of makeup like oranges against his face, he continued: "It's not I don't like it. It's that I rebelled against the message."

"Take it easy," she said.

"No, no, I'm not upset, but listen to the words. I mean, did you ever listen to the words? You know, 'Hurt me, baby, hurt me; the more you hurt me the more I love you.' Remember 'Cry Baby'?"

"Little Anthony and the Imperials."

"A song in which tears are about to be shed; and you know it because eyes get red."

Theresa acted as if she hadn't heard him, staring determinedly at the shoulder of his jacket.

"It's hopeless, don't you see what I mean? Sure there's some joy in the fast songs, I guess, but it's pimp music. It's suffering. It's hopeless." His voice trailed off.

"It's just a song."

"It's not just a song; it's an attitude to life."

And the song that was playing seemed so unhappy and familiar that David had to keep talking not to be overwhelmed. "It was a thematic rebellion," he said, not vehement any more.

Theresa swung him around, her chunky body surprisingly strong as she took the lead, as if she was pushing him off topic.

"I mean, what good's that stuff on Sunday afternoons?" David kept going. "Remember how we'd play records? Then what? Christ, Toronto. It was like Belfast. What a bleak time."

"There's Pat." Theresa turned him again. "Haven't you been waiting to see her? Your first girlfriend." She said it without malice or sentimentality.

At first talking to Pat was almost the same as talking to Theresa. They were both the same size, and Pat was just as oblique, turning her head aside and rolling her eyes. But Pat was friendlier, and David sensed she'd drop the evasive, distancing, practical baby voice they both used much faster than Theresa would. Defensively lively, Pat joked about things like plastic surgery – "Cheekbone implants? I'll have two of those, please."

"Come on. You look great."

"Tummy tucks? I'll have one of those as well."

"Ah, don't. How do you keep looking so good?"

"Young men." She laughed.

In the indistinct light at the edge of the dance floor, and because she wore a lot of eye shadow, Pat's face, with real high cheekbones, seemed to David to be smudged, hidden behind smoke. Maybe it was the darker colour in her hair, he thought. As she took out the picture of her boyfriend and David leaned close to her to look at it, he could sense her warmth. It wasn't perfume, or the smell of her hair; just warmth.

No, she wasn't married, no, no kids; she worked for a textile company in Montreal and travelled a lot; it *wasn't* hard on her; she did have a niece: "And she seems such a baby, playing with makeup, and she's the same age I was when I was with you." Accusatory, yet strangely tentative, Pat tilted her head and waited for a reply.

David felt blindsided. It had obviously taken an effort for Pat to refer to this part of their past, but as she confronted him she also looked curious, as if watching an experiment.

Ashamed, David realized – it seemed for the first time – that someone else could feel as deeply as he did without expressing it in the same way: without talking incessantly about every thought that entered his head. And his instant openness, with Theresa, with Pat, had been overbearing.

"Those things you showed me," she prodded.

That gave him an opening. He could have argued and evaded and said "we did those things together"; he could have focussed on the oblique way she referred to their having been lovers: they'd "been together" – she almost lisped! He could have said "I didn't know it hurt you so much." David kept silent. What Pat was referring to wasn't really their first time together, but an act so ugly and cruel he couldn't remember all the details. But he did remember chasing her outside afterwards, then all he could recall was the dead light of early dark on Jameson Avenue, not Pat. The cold and the streetlights on at four o'clock. He also remembered the light in Mitchell's apartment, all the drapes drawn against winter darkness making it worse. There was another excuse for what he'd done: Mitchell, poor Mitchell, who'd sniffed so much glue he'd found first Buddha, then Jehovah, and wound up with a shaved head on a dialysis machine. Mitchell, with his boxing and dead father in North Bay and mother who worked at Thompson's Dry Cleaners. She smelled of solvent. Her boyfriend's name was Larry.

A lie. An excuse. Mitchell hadn't even been there that day, or if he had he didn't figure in what happened. And David had never smelled Mitchell's mother. All he could remember were the clean white blouses she wore in the store; she was dumpy and friendly with thin red lips. David himself hadn't been sniffing glue that day either, nor had the three men he had let sit in the bedroom closet and watch while he made love to Pat. One of them couldn't stand it; he came out. David had wound up wrestling on the floor with him, naked. Pat grabbed her clothes and rushed away. Now he remembered, he made himself remember.

The border of Pat's beige slip; how had she held it? Her hand. The other boy squeezing his genitals while David held him in a headlock. David made himself face every detail he could. How dim it was in that room! The only light in the apartment hung over the dining room table, far away. The other man had wanted to "meet him outside" and David changed into Mitchell's hard-toed shoes to be able to kick better – only there hadn't been any fight. Talking to Pat, and even at the time it was strange to him: her not seeming too affected. Just because she was silent.

"That time in Mitchell's apartment," he said. "I didn't know what it meant. I mean I did, but what it could do. I didn't realize…"

"I still think about it." She didn't hesitate.

"It was insane." Tearing up, unexpectedly, David said, "It's no excuse."

"There, there," she said.

"I didn't think. I mean, I must have known, but…"

"It was horrifying."

She'd been so quiet in Mitchell's hall, leaning against the door and stepping forward into her skirt while he talked – as if he could make up for what he'd done by cajoling!

"It was ugly," he said.

"I had to face those people every day. It affected my whole life. It's not something you forget."

And he didn't forget what had followed as inevitably as night follows day: wanting her back and yearning and disbelief at how totally she could reject him. The theme was as predictable as the song that was playing: I didn't realize what I had in you until I lost you. Yet the whole cycle of longing he went through didn't seem to have any place for what he'd actually done. But then, standing there, thinking how inappropriate it was that she should be comforting him, a strange displacement that had never happened before. The dark cavern of the convention centre disappeared and it was as though he was seeing through water to a summer sky long ago. Pat and her girlfriend were by a bench near a red sandstone Victorian school building, and David saw how Pat had looked at him for the first time. And he saw her friend, Sandy, so dark and with such a white smile, strange and stunning with her black black hair.

Northern Lake Huron, somewhere David had hardly heard of, and never been, was where Sandy came from; that's about all she'd say, except that her brother worked on the lake boats. She was evasive. Yet David thought of rocks and blue water – could it have been from books he'd seen as a child? Images came: a steel hull in cold water, a ship far out on the only lake he knew, Ontario.

Pat was from Minaki, a place David had *never* heard of, but she wasn't as elusive as Sandy. Years later David found out that Sandy was Ojibway, but she'd hidden it completely. She hid everything behind that smile, though he knew her brother never did come back and she had no father. Pat had no father; her mother lived with someone else. David had no father, Mitchell had no father; no one seemed to have a father. Where the playground stretched vacant in front of them to the street he could see the yellow brick high rises of Jameson Avenue. The buildings, indifferent as cliffs, guarded them in some way, the same buildings for which an entire neighbourhood had been destroyed, and which David hated, but they were the reason they'd met. There was no other place for the new children to live.

They always came together in the early evenings after that, the cobalt sky so different from the dead macabre days with nothing, *nothing* to do. There were no jobs, no cottages; he and Mitchell might visit and sit as time passed. They yearned for something, and walked down to the lake to be near water; only to stare at still flotsam behind the breakwater. Once, becoming again disturbed, violent children, they played hunting, and Mitchell killed a sparrow with his BB gun. David, astonishing even Mitchell, tasted its blood, touching a bright bead in the corner of the dead eye with the tip of his tongue. All that wild wounding. Boredom, adolescence, emptiness.

Alone one time, at the Exhibition grounds, David crawled into the cupola of a building, sitting in the must and timbers. It was as if he had climbed into his own tomb to die, smelling the mould, a very small boy waiting for a monster to come and kill him; it was profoundly sexual. And yet that same night, after supper, wearing a clean shirt and walking Pat home, he seemed as far away as it was possible to be from the morbid wraith of the afternoon. In Minaki, she happily told him, everyone was afraid of bears when it started to get dark, "especially if you were near the dump." Bears were truly frightening, he believed it, but they were fear of a different order. As he'd sat stunned and excited in his hiding place, old oak leaves rustling on the floor when he moved, cold coming in from the windows above, he'd seemed to cultivate a sense of not existing; now he was so alive he panicked. How could he have been his earlier self? That twilight the sky flashed green, tropical for a moment, just as the sun set; darkness came quickly. Fall was near. He kissed Pat.

In a joking, accepting way, David became part of Pat's family. Sandy and her secrets seemed to disappear. Whenever David went to Pat's apartment her mother had a way of kidding him that made his enthusiasm about where they came from, about the north, somehow dignified. Once he'd told them about his interest David couldn't control himself, almost as if he had to spoil it by talking it to death. They stopped him; they laughed, a little uncomfortably because he was so intense; they took him seriously.

When David had been at a Catholic school he'd been fascinated by stories of the Jesuit martyrs. At first it was the grotesqueries of the torture, lovingly delineated by Brother Xavier, who then smashed the face of any boy who admitted to going steady. But below the horrific, the psychotic priests, the "savages," David had a sense of a country where he lived that no one knew about. There had been a forest here, and Iroquois; not a remnant remained. And when he shared his near dream with Pat, and told her mother, when he talked obsessively about this almost imaginative green place, they seemed to know what he was yearning for.

On a family trip to Niagara Falls, which seemed to have been arranged for David, they stopped at the gorge and Pat's mother told him to climb down, "go on, go get your bush." Pat went with him. Another time, again on a trip they seemed to have planned as some kind of "cure" for him, they joked that staying in a cabin at Wasaga Beach "wasn't Elliot Lake." But David had a sense there, just a glimpse – the paperboard partition with Pat sleeping on the other side, sand on the linoleum and on the rag carpet, raw wet cedar between the buildings – of something wild. They laughed some more, and shared what he felt.

He'd killed it all. Even when he knew that Pat had given him an inestimable gift. David sensed how wrong things were when men sneered at what they wanted most, and how different it had been the first time with Pat. It didn't affect how he would end up acting. The very cupola where he had felt urged to stop existing didn't matter – he actually forgot he'd ever been in it – when he walked past the cupola with Pat and held her: the leaden sky spread out behind them wide as all the world. His hysterical cruelty had not even been slowed. All that remained was the ability to mythologize.

"You know, the first job I ever had up north I drove from Dryden to Minaki to see where you lived."

"The road wasn't paved back then."

"I went back again just last year, and I asked about you."

"Same old David."

"I asked about your family. Are you native? I mean like Sandy."

"It'd be news to my mother."

"This guy at the store told me—"

"Does it matter?" She looked up at him, challenged him.

"No."

"Come with me," and he followed her off the dark dance floor and into the bright lights of the lobby.

As he squinted she turned to face him again.

"You know, I don't regret relationships."

He looked at her and saw clearly what had happened. Sentimentality faded. They couldn't have stayed together, but with Pat he'd touched a force that seemed to spread through other lives like a tree. It also died, but with her, for a moment, everything had been alive. Wind rattled the black glass high above: there was his damaged life, his terrible regret. There was affection and love abiding.